D0223994

death, the one and the art of theatre

Howard Barker's first book of theatre theory, *Arguments for a Theatre*, established his reputation as a thinker as well as a practitioner of his own Theatre of Catastrophe. In this new book, he extends his engagement with tragedy to identify the source of its authority in its profound engagement with death. Barker's now-famous aphorism 'I do not know the theatre and the theatre does not know me' is the starting point for this controversial statement of artistic faith, which includes his articulation of the principles governing what he calls 'the art of theatre' as well as a meditation on love and its pathological obsession with 'the one . . .'.

Born in London in 1946, playwright Howard Barker's early work was performed at the Royal Court and the RSC, and later by The Wrestling School, the English theatre company formed in 1988 to focus exclusively on the presentation of Barker's texts. Now a poet and dramatist of international renown, his plays are performed widely throughout the US and Europe. His best-known works include *Victory*, *The Castle*, *Scenes from an Execution* and *Gertrude – The Cry*.

death, the one and the art of theatre

Howard Barker

Routledge
Taylor & Francis Group

LONDON AND NEW YORK

First published 2005
by Routledge
2 Park Square, Milton Park, Abingdon, Oxon OX14 4RN

Simultaneously published in the USA and Canada
by Routledge
270 Madison Ave, New York, NY 10016

Routledge is an imprint of the Taylor & Francis Group

© 2005 Howard Barker

Typeset in Melior
by Keystroke, Jacaranda Lodge, Wolverhampton
Printed and bound in Great Britain
by TJ International Ltd, Padstow, Cornwall

All rights reserved. No part of this book may be reprinted
or reproduced or utilized in any form or by any
electronic, mechanical, or other means, now known or
hereafter invented, including photocopying and recording,
or in any information storage or retrieval system, without
permission in writing from the publishers.

British Library Cataloguing in Publication Data
A catalogue record for this book is available from the British Library

Library of Congress Cataloging in Publication Data
Barker, Howard.
    Death, the one and the art of theatre / Howard Barker.
        p. cm.
1. Barker, Howard—Authorship.   2. Barker, Howard—Aesthetics.
3. Theater—Philosophy.   4. Death in literature.
5. Drama—Technique.   6. Love in literature.   7. Playwriting.
I. Title.
    PR6052.A6485Z464 2004
    822′.914—dc22   2004012119

ISBN 0–415–34986–9 (hbk)
ISBN 0–415–34987–7 (pbk)

For Judith Burns

I do not know *the theatre*, and *the theatre* does not know me.

❋

There is *the theatre* and there is *the art of theatre*. All that is proposed in this book pertains to the latter.

❋

Some have had to do with *the art of theatre*, but finding it too arduous, chose to join *the theatre*. These are legion. A few remained faithful. Very few, because it is a painful path.

❋

The theatre purports to give pleasure to the many. *The art of theatre* lends anxiety to the few. Which is the greater gift?

❋

Nothing *said* about death by the living can possibly relate to death as it will be experienced by the dying. Nothing *known* about death by the dead can be communicated to the living. Over this appalling chasm tragedy throws a frail bridge of imagination.

❋

Since theatre ceased to make death its subject it surrendered its authority over the human soul. Since it allowed itself to be incorporated into mundane projects of political indoctrination and social therapy it abdicated its power. Always theatre is suborned by the idealism of its makers. Always it is traduced by the sentimental. In *the art of theatre* we pity the idealist as one pities the man with a fatal disease. This pity is strictly circumscribed. Whilst many have tried to make hospitals from theatres we keep our stage infection-free.

●

All I describe is theatre even where theatre is not the subject.

●

One has heard talk of many theatres existing, and of many forms, as if theatres tolerated one another. The fact is that theatres annihilate one another as all religions annihilate one another. Is this because theatre is a religion? Let us confess, *the art of theatre* has many of the characteristics of religion. For example, it finds so much theatre *anathema*. It *excommunicates*. Its methods are akin to *prayer*. What distinguishes it from all religion is this, however: that it recoils from *truth*. It repudiates *truth* as vulgarity.

●

All cultures are enslaved by idealism – they are defined by their servitude to the ideal. Only tragedy locates the ideal in death, but because death is the first enemy of political systems, tragedy is caricatured as *negativity*. The bravery of tragedy – where not even sexual love is sufficient to abolish the fascination of death – lies in its refutation of pleasure as an organizing principle of existence. Who would deny that this contempt for pleasure is also an ecstasy?

⁂

The theatre is often contrasted with the street, as if it were false, and the street real. *The art of theatre* asserts its absolute independence of the street. It values the door. It values the wall. It leaves the street to the street. In any case, who says the street is real? It *pretends* to be real. The fact so many persist in the fiction that it is real is of no concern to us.

⁂

Silence is the consequence of too-deep knowledge in some, of ignorance in others.

⁂

The dread of speech is a sign of spiritual health, for the banality of speech is universal and induces nausea. In *the*

3

art of theatre we acknowledge a solitary obligation – *to save speech from itself.*

❋

To tell the truth sincerely is the pitiful pretension of the theatre. To lie sincerely is the euphoria of *the art of theatre.*

❋

To ask for truth in theatre is contradictory, a repudiation of its essence. Consequently, death, a subject for which true statements are, a priori, inadmissible, is the subject most perfectly suited to the form of theatre.

❋

We are not born full of sin, we are born full of the appetite for it.

❋

We repudiate all those who find theatre *congenial. The art of theatre* is constructed on the premiss that the creation of happiness is no part of its function. Nor does it have a *function.*

❋

To seduce this woman and not another. To seduce this man and not another. We are faintly discriminating.

●

To move continually out of reach. To be only ever *proximate*.

●

I come close. I tell *everything*. But only in such a way that the listener wonders if what he heard was *imagined*.

●

Confession is also discretion. '*Why did I fail to include the fact that I . . .?*'

●

To seduce this woman and not another. To seduce this man and not another. The influence of the locality. The charm of coincidence. The failure to exploit (the dropped handkerchief, the entire store of stratagems). The seducer's nausea at his own propositions. The prospect of having to admit nothing turned out as planned.

●

When the light came on, he saw her face was disfigured. This had the effect of extinguishing his desire. He found an excuse to avoid the consequences of what he himself had initiated. His actions were, however, dictated by consideration of a purely *public* kind. It was not in his sexuality that he experienced offence. On the contrary, he sensed his erotic instinct was enhanced by her disfigurement ('*what or who had so damaged her? How had she inspired such mistreatment?*'). Once he was able to acknowledge this he accepted the challenge of her condition. He nevertheless stipulated she wore tighter clothes.

●

All I describe is theatre even where theatre is not the subject.

●

So essential is theatre to *the idea of life* it cannot be compromised by making itself *the imitation of life*. It cannot be humiliated by rituals of reproduction.

●

The theatre reproduces life. *The art of theatre* invents life. This act of invention may be perceived as a critique of the poverty of existence. It is not *social criticism*.

●

The art of theatre, in its impatience with the world, utters in its own languages. Moreover, it understands these languages to be the means by which its public is *cleansed* of the detritus of familiarity, domesticity and recognition.

The art of theatre was fear-inspiring. The Humanists, who know of no *use* for fear, nor can imagine the sublimity of fear, abolished it from the stage. We talk, however, of theatre as crucially an art of death. We assert the dominance of fear in the life of the characters. In this we are, paradoxically, realists.

Death is the preoccupation of great art even where it is not the *subject* of it. When the utilitarians seized the theatre death simply stood in the foyer, as patient as a chauffeur.

To enter the space silently. To enter it thinking of death. To make death the whole subject even when laughter discloses the ambiguity of our passions. To *admit* death.

To *admit death* . . . to know *now* what you knew but were denied consciousness of . . . that *all* is predicated on death . . . is this political?

❋

What is the function of laughter in tragedy? Can we talk of a function in tragedy? Let us put it another way: how does laughter serve the experience of tragedy? By implicating us in its seductive process. It is a dropped handkerchief.

❋

The peculiar laugh of tragedy. The laugh on the rim of death.

❋

The dropped handkerchief: accident/intention/the beauty of a falling thing/white is a sign/I surrender/ intimate as underwear/to retrieve it is to begin/ impossible not to retrieve it/an obligation/excuse me/we both know/this will perhaps be fatal.

❋

The foyer is not neutral. Always the play of death is at war with the foyer. The foyer is *the theatre* par excellence. It is the first aim of *the art of theatre* to abolish the foyer.

●

Cruelty is cheap, like philanthropy.

●

We should all like to choose our deaths, both the moment and the manner. We should like to control this as all the episodes of life. But death is not an episode of life, it is beyond life and nothing that pertains to life pertains to death. It was the same with the birth agony. We were coming into a place. With death we are going into a place. Or, if we are not going into a place, certainly we are leaving one . . .

●

The sexual moment is not a knowing. Its vitality is nevertheless inspired by the misapprehension that it is a knowing, as all exploration purports to be knowing, as all journeys proclaim their knowing. The well-travelled are notoriously ignorant.

●

The ancient element of violence in the wedding is dimly visible in the tears the mother sheds for the bride. These tears are commonly misunderstood as tears of joy, in the way a culture of gratification converts every manifestation of pain into the substance of its own sentimentality. But are these tears not tears of pity inspired by the spectacle of a beauty contrived solely for its own violation?

●

Speaking of those one might have loved, we like to indulge a spurious melancholy. The experience of life seems reducible to missed opportunities, near-encounters, appointments that failed to materialize. Thus we can comfort ourselves with another false-tragedy, that So-and-So, with whom we were destined to live a life of passion, somehow evaded us, that the objective situation conspired to obstruct a critical encounter. We are thus delivered into the power of the arbitrary, a pretext, a self-justification for spoiled life. If, conversely, the loved one need not have been the *only one* (a nauseating exclusivity according to democratic ideology, where absolute interchangeability is the rule) but rather the world is profuse with possibility, the arbitrary becomes the excellent, a condition of luxury. Certainly, if it is true that by failing to be in a certain place one relinquished *one* love, the opposite must equally apply, that by being in another place one delivered oneself to the possibility of encountering *another* . . .

All I describe is theatre even where theatre is not the subject.

•

Kiss carefully – not an admonition about kissing, an act of banality/an act of terrible depth, but about the *kissed one*.

•

The clumsiness of all theatre where the artist is not ignorant. The poverty of all text where the dramatist is not ignorant. How can we speak of ignorance as a virtue? Because we are nauseated by the *knowing*. Because we long to share the ordeal of the *unknowing*, who alone possess a beautiful intention.

•

The paradox that we require bad art to make us long for a testament of authenticity. What do we mean by authenticity? Not a *true account* (let the journalists account truthfully, i.e. not at all) but a spectacle of utterance, the utterance born of an ordeal.

•

11

Her dread he would say the same things. Her relief that he *did* say the same things. Her contempt that he said them . . .

•

The demonstration causes me to ask not what was demonstrated but who is the demonstrator?

•

When we are ordered to be free are we entitled to ask in whose interest should we be free? In the existing state of language, never mind ethics, it is not self-evident that freedom is a gift.

•

Why do you require me to be free?

•

The photographic paper before its immersion in the developing tank. The invisible is present. The immanent form. But never an immutable form (we might stop the development . . . the exhaustion of the chemicals . . .).

•

The old photograph. What is behind the tree? Something was behind the tree. To turn the photograph on its edge. To scratch away the surface of the tree.

*

The land behind the tree continues. A field, leading to a road. The road leads to the city. At this moment (the moment of the photograph) in the city, a room where a woman (a man) crosses one leg over the other. This is both contained in and excluded from the photograph. The essential *agony* of all photography.

*

Where this photograph was taken (the place) may never have changed (we cannot identify the place). Whilst few places are unchanged, we cannot say authoritatively that the general law of change applies to *this place*. So the photograph has the status of a wound, which smarts with its *irresolution* . . .

*

Profound emotional experiences even where they fill the audience with despair (perceived 'negativity') serve to increase resistance to social coercion (the more so since all social coercion justifies itself on the pleasure principle). The pessimistic work of art – who dares talk of death as pessimism? – strengthens the observer by obliging him to include death in his categories of thought. How do we sense the infinite value of death as the subject of artistic undertakings? By reference to the hostility shown to it by authoritarians and democrats alike, who identify it as inimical to their collectivist projects. This alone endows it with charm, even – *vitality* . . .

●

Not understanding the point. The ecstasy of vanishing meaning. Hiding in plethora. In the forest of concepts a pure stream.

●

Desire increased in inverse proportion to revelation. Desire as a state of ignorance. We demand so little of the desired one.

●

The eternal quality in hatred. It cannot be extinguished, it merely migrates. Does this depress you?

●

Even the optimists do not want to inhabit paradise. Paradise is only coercion. The optimist is a cynic. This is always revealed by his sense of humour.

❋

The Good Samaritan was reluctant. He expected to be robbed by the man he helped. He fought to overcome this reluctance. When he found he was not the victim of a trick he experienced relief, and this relief was far greater than any pleasure he felt in knowing himself to be kind.

❋

The profound misery of Don Juan. The nauseating sense that a given sequence of words and gestures would secure an effect. The slow substitution therefore of cruelty for love, a will to *inflict* himself on others, when the self-same phrases had once been a plea for peace, for revelation . . .

❋

The word. This word, which is only this word and not another. There is an ocean of vocabulary and in it shoals of approximations but only this word has the power to annihilate all others. This certainty of the word, which enters its place uncontested, is the divine quality in speaking, is characteristic of *the speech* and never present in conversation.

❋

The art of theatre abolishes the conversation . . .

❋

To make dignities of one's obsessions. To invest in a proclivity thought unworthy of investment . . .

❋

The blush. Its complexities and contradictions. Its apparent tenderness, its actual revelation of violence, sacrifice and the abyss.

❋

On the roads and beneath the roads. In the fields and under them. The profusion of relics. But the absence of the relic does not inhibit speculation.

❋

All I describe is theatre even where theatre is not the subject.

16

They made love on a field track. They remained standing. The landscape was therefore in the act, perhaps the cause of the act. She wished to become pregnant by the act. This desire to be pregnant owed more to the landscape than to the lover, his power, his charm, etcetera, notwithstanding. This landscape was a cruel one, broken and flooded. A nearly dark sky hung over them. Everything was redolent of loss, poverty and abandon. They took this pain into the embrace.

*

The theatre prefers the easy way because the audience prefers the easy way, and *the theatre* defers to the audience; it is, in every sense, *made from it*. Of those few who repudiate the easy way, fewer still can tolerate the silence of the audience. They receive it as a wound. In *the art of theatre* not only do we expect the audience to be silent, we demand it of them, we demand it as the confirmation of our intentions. We concede there are many silences, but we *discriminate* among the silences.

*

There were many reasons not to love the loved one. Above all, the difficulty of loving her, such that he would cry out in his frustration, '*this is not worth the trouble*'.

Nevertheless, the more trouble he went to, the more he was gratified by the few moments of love that were *not* troublesome. He persuaded himself their passion was cursed, only in order to feel brave in defying the curse . . .

●

How should we enter death? Is this not the subject of all philosophy and all theatre, despite the protestations of all philosophy and all theatre that they are instruments for *living*?

●

We go to the tragedy to know what we already know, what we have known since birth, that our lives are dedicated to death, a knowledge all other forms of social existence contrive to conceal from us, with our connivance. Tragedy was attacked so long as death was attacked, a state of affairs so preposterous it could not last, a state of affairs induced by a reckless, blind and alcoholic rationalism . . .

●

The youth entered the theatre where a voice announced the cancellation of the performance. At first he was relieved because as with all assignations with the unknown he had experienced an apprehension that he might not enjoy the encounter (there were rumours about the play, which when he thought about it, reminded him of rumours he had heard about 'cruel' women . . .). But a short while after, still in the auditorium where no performance was taking place (he had no other place to go), he grew resentful, because having braced himself for the ordeal, he now felt *deprived* of it. He recognized in himself a secret longing to suffer from the exposure to unknown life, even to be *damaged* by it . . .

●

Everything you know and strive to know was already known to the dead – or is known to them. Are we diminished by this?

●

The cool of the morning. I sit in a field, rinsed by the scents of the flora. A hare travels home over the furrows. I am consumed by a sense of intimacy with the world, the self disintegrated, a dissolution therefore, but also a belonging. The dead have known this, and some knew not only this but *precisely* this. Am I diminished?

●

The play only appears to be about the living because the actors are living. The *characters* have never lived, nor by the same token, can they ever be said to be *dead*. Theatre is situated on the bank of the Styx (the side of the living). The actually dead cluster at the opposite side, begging to be recognized. What is it they have to tell? Their mouths gape . . .

●

Very great plays yield no meanings. They move like the mouths of the dead on the banks of the Styx. 'Meaningful' plays are soiled/spoiled by their meanings. What is the *meaning* of death?

●

The loved one shared all his emotions and all his attitudes. Is this too rash an assertion? He didn't think so. When they encountered an individual or experienced an event it was certain that one look would pass between them which in itself contained the entire volume of their unanimity ('*what an idiot*', '*I can't take any more of this*', '*he is lying through his teeth*' and so on . . .). If anyone was *the* one, it was she. Yet for all the exemplification of accord that the loved one represented, he was aware she was not *the one* at all. He sensed, with a terrible fore-boding, that mutuality was not a sign of *the one*, that any amount of agreement was *beside the point*, as a marching and chanting crowd is also a symbol of frailty and deception . . .

*

In stating that all I describe is theatre even where theatre is not the subject am I asserting theatre is / is like life? Emphatically not.

*

To become dead is to cease the elaboration of values, the prioritization of values, the valuing of values.

*

The plague house is a site of terror to the undying and the dying alike, but this assessment of it is a characteristic of the living, a fact of *discrimination* (evaluation, association, preference). For the dying, discrimination ebbs with the ebbing of life. At a certain point in the life of the dying the disgust of the plague house has no more meaning than the charm of the honeysuckle garden one had always aspired to *cease* in . . .

*

In Christian culture the apology is the last act of life, as apology characterizes the Christian life in all its moments.

Beyond the Christian era we can no longer be satisfied with the apology as the precondition for entering death. We can only go into death with a contempt of life, with a sense of life's poverty. Without God we may dare to say life is not worthy of *us*.

•

Tragedy is the labour of death. Whereas the labour of birth is characterized by hope, in the labour of death hope is discarded at the outset as a distraction, an irrelevance. In tragedy the hopeful character is at best comic, at worst contemptible.

•

The recognition of *the one* comes in the form of the conspiracy. The origins of the conspiracy have the usual signs of erotic transaction (glances / too many glances / the blush / proximity) but immediately assume an exclusive character, one shaped by *negativity* ('*you are not that sort, surely?*'). In this triumph of distinction, the world is simultaneously annexed ('*our place*') and abolished (a sordid territory populated by the livers of poorer life . . .)

•

Only when *the one* had ceased to be recognizable solely as *desire* but had taken on the characteristics of a *need* did vast hinterlands of irreconcilable difference reveal themselves. It was as if great landlords shared a road that ran between their estates, but these estates were put to vastly different uses. He watched her misunderstand him. She sensed he was able to exist without her. *The one* was only sometimes *the one*. The remainder of the time was spent in drawing the one into the *state of one-ness*. Yet could this fragility of *one-ness* not serve as its definition?

The theatre – why did the moralists collect there? Why had they always brought their gnawing missions to the stage, and why were they so enraged when *the art of theatre* revealed its aesthetic incompatibility with morality? (It did not stoop to *repudiate* what in any case was *alien* to it, a fundamental *contradiction*.)

He walked out of the hospital and into the grounds. Whereas death held no horror for him, sickness did, so the very staircases and their odours, the colour of the walls – the ugliness of which served as yet further evidence of the refusal of the healthy to contemplate the sick – caused him to retch. He had instructions enabling him to penetrate the maze of temporary buildings in order to discover the mortuary. Steam pipes sneaked everywhere, some of great diameter carried overhead in conduits. Nothing possessed any order, or if it had order, it had no *plan*, planning being a mark of will or even love, and sickness calls forth neither in men. Weeds rose in great density around a wooden stair. A door of such poor manufacture that its plywood curled back upon itself opened into a room where he saw the body at once, small-faced and under a shroud tucked hastily under the chin. A man of foreign origin greeted him. He wore a short white coat, hardly clean. He tactfully withdrew, exaggerating his solicitude. The dead man was not himself, it went without saying, but those features that still showed signs of that self were altered, shrunken or parodied. The eyes were not entirely closed. There was an overwhelming sense of rejection, discarding and abandon, and nothing of repose. The dead man had left himself, a litter in a wretched hut. So he kissed that, for there was nothing better to kiss . . .

❋

All I describe is theatre even where theatre is not the subject.

❋

Nothing knowable is not already known. The problem is to create the conditions under which the knowable might make itself known, should one wish to know it. To know more, we must violate ourselves more. We must violate our own secret. As for '*the open mind*', what is that but a complacency of egotists?

❦

The philosopher Mosca identifies 187 meanings which might be derived from the words 'I love you'. Of these, 100 are statements of indifference, 63 of hatred.

❦

On certain days it is intolerable that a blackbird can sing from the roof of a murderer. On others, it is the most perfect expression of existence.

❦

In *the art of theatre* we recoil from the idea of satisfaction, either of the public or of ourselves. Satisfaction derives from resolution. Nothing in *the art of theatre* tends towards resolution. We elevate anxiety over all things but *beauty*.

❦

In *the art of theatre* beauty is characterized by its brevity, its instability, its *ill-health*. Whereas death is the nightmare of cheerless democracies, abolished from consciousness by the nauseating complicity of medicine and leisure, death in *the art of theatre* is the condition of beauty and anxiety the price of its revelation. Would you be seduced effortlessly?

●

Who would choose to experience anxiety when
　　　Life is hard enough as it is?
　　For the same money we might forget our troubles in
　　　another place?
Only those whose souls recoil from *deathlessness* . . .

●

Only *the one* is capable of drawing you from the abyss into which she has plunged you. Conversely, were she not capable of consigning you to the abyss she could not be *the one* . . .

●

Precisely because
　　　Life is hard enough as it is
　　For the same money we might forget our troubles in
　　　another place
The art of theatre repudiates *the deal*. Must we entice you from your complacency?

＊

We say a cruel man has a soul when he contemplates the
contradictions of his cruelty. Should we not extend this
criterion to the merciful?

＊

Because *the art of theatre* is a sacred art it belongs to
actors but not to *entertainers*. The actor entering *the art
of theatre* must know it might cost him his life. Who
would risk his life to be an *entertainer*? How distaste-
ful it would be to execute a conjuror, a comic, a fakir; it
would be an act of wanton excess (even had he stolen
your wife). Of no entertainer could it be said his enter-
tainment earned him his punishment. But an actor,
him you might justly indict with having *broken your
world* . . .

＊

The poet was dying in his room, the identical room he
had been born in, wept in, seduced in, experienced sickness in, thought nothing at all in. Some poets consider
it their duty to travel to distant places. He believed in the
opposite, that a poet ought never to move. This discipline
was however impossible to maintain against the powers
of his curiosity. He had been lured to great cities, even
while he wrote bitterly of these infringements of his rule,

fervently denying his poetry had been freshened by the change and insisting it was the fact of his immersion in a single place that had enabled him to produce his greatest lines. He affirmed the struggle of the poet was not to extend the range of his familiarity but to go deeper, to *sink beneath*. Of course he sensed the terror of this tunnelling; for example an appalling hatred flooded him at one stage, and whilst he did not repudiate this hatred but regarded it as one more constituent of the strata of his own geology, he passed gratefully through it to cooler places and colder thought. Now at last he was dying, and in this room which however known was still not fully known and possibly not *fully knowable*. The paradox that filled his dying was therefore this: whether death had arrived because he was about to violate his own last secret and the very poverty of this secret could only have ridiculed his entire existence, or whether on the contrary he was poised to violate a secret so profound that life had summoned death to obstruct his extraordinary enlightenment. In his crisis it was still not evident to him whether he had lived for *nothing* (an absurd chemistry) or *something* (no category he could define . . .).

●

The one observed him through narrowed eyes. He had disappointed her and she did nothing to conceal this disappointment. Because he knew there were no reasonable grounds for this disappointment he was unwilling to dignify it by discussing its causes. Thus it sprawled between them like a lifeless animal. A simpler man might have argued for his right *not to be a disappointment* but he sensed *the one required* to be disappointed, that possibly her demeanour, her whole attitude to existence, was defined by it and that it constituted not only her beauty but the substance of her *one-ness* . . .

●

He could state with honesty that in the case of *the one* he never knew what to expect. How this volatility contributed to or detracted from her suitability to be *the one* interested him in an almost clinical way. Certainly love thrives on surprise, and he had in any case a certain liking for his own pain, thinking it an antidote to permanent affability. On the other hand, her apparent indifference to his feelings caused him to despise her, implying as it did a coarse and even brutal sensibility. It was as if she disqualified herself by the revelation of those very characteristics that had so stimulated his desire in the first place. Thus when she announced she had fallen in love with another man he laughed. And it was not hollow, this laugh. Whilst it was a convenient resolution to his dilemma, what he found ridiculous in her confession was the discovery she had found the capacity to love another man when to love him could – had she been *the one* – only have wholly absorbed her emotional resources. When he saw her face was marked by anger at his laughter, he decided (it was a *decision*) to despise her for that also . . .

•

Death is the limit not only of life but also of imagination and therefore the stop of poetry, for whereas poetry is so often concerned with death it is effectively about life's regret for death. We are fond of asserting we can imagine anything, and it is obvious one need never have done a thing, or witnessed its occurrence, to imagine it (the shocking authority of dreams, the peculiar authenticity of works of art where no artist ever *saw* the subject) but we cannot imagine the state of death – it is, along with infinity, impossible to envisage, and where death or the after-life has been represented artistically the poverty of its representation only serves to demonstrate the absurdity of the effort. A genius of Dante's stature, or a Bosch, produces inane pictures of the heavenly condition and equally comic images of hell. The unknown is evoked by reference to the known, a legitimate practice of the metaphorist, but in this instance alone, a *failed equation* . . .

•

Nevertheless, like the gnawing of an irrepressible sexual hunger, the need to imagine death steals over us, and in the form of a *fascination* (what cannot be done must be done/what cannot be said must be said/what cannot be entered will be entered). This fascination is falsely described as *morbid* . . .

❀

The value of *the fence* . . . the ecstasy of *denial* . . . where all is accessible, the beauty of *the ban* . . . where all is revealed, *the secret* . . .

❀

A place (intellectual, actual) closed *for no reason* . . .

❀

The inevitability of the seduction of the Vestal Virgins, but the only suitable punishment for their seduction – death. The penalty worth the offence, *a price worth paying* (or so it *seemed*, for not-knowing-death to evaluate the gamble is impossible, and whereas one can imagine the ecstasy of seduction, one cannot imagine the scale of death's cruelty . . . if it *is* cruel . . . or its kindness . . . if it *is* kind . . .).

❀

The art of theatre is a rehearsal for death but more, a confession of ignorance, of the limits of knowledge . . .

What greater testimony to the gesture of tragedy than the contempt of its adversaries? The rationalists cling to their fallacies like drowning men. What is the most preposterous of these fallacies? That *all is knowable*. How death enrages them . . . ! Is it surprising they wish to abolish it?

Tragedy is *hope-less*. Death is *hope-less*. Neither is bereft of hope, rather they have *dispensed* with hope. They exist in a vortex, not of *hopelessness* ('the situation is hope-less' always contains the plea for a miracle) but a vortex without categories either of optimism or pessimism. Who would say tragedy is pessimistic? Only a fool, for the tragic gesture demands the abolition of pessimism at the outset, it identifies it as a *redundancy*, along with its opposite.

Hope-lessness is the point of departure, not a closure but a new condition . . .

The art of theatre aspires to a moral nakedness. It is the antithesis of education therefore, which is clothing, which is a suffocation in *ethical garments*.

The theatre trades in relief, it dispenses cheap medicines, among them, *irony*. The obverse of tragedy is not comedy, which by virtue of its cruelty lives in tragedy also, but *irony* . . .

The art of theatre takes pain as its subject, not to exploit it for political ends, as a lesson in moral obligations but as *an end in itself* . . .

Pain is mesmerizing, let us admit it. The tragic protagonist observes her own pain without *asking to be saved*. Saved for what? For more of this life? But she has already repudiated this life . . . ! This is the secret intelligence of the tragic experience, that the world is inadequate. Without this recognition, how can she negotiate her own death?

Tragedy does not stoop to *hate life*, for *loving life* and *hating life* are equally infantile, the philosophical equivalent of a nursery rhyme. Tragedy has *no opinion* . . .

Death communicates nothing. To describe it as mute is to speak only part of its mystery. It is not to be found on the surface of the cadaver (however one strains to make meaning from the cadaver, it yields nothing, it *resists* meaning, or if it owns a vocabulary we do not know it) . . .

Death is not in the remains . . .

Tragedy, like death, is concerned with what is not self-evident (the cadaver is not *death*, only the detritus of death . . .).

Idealism and cynicism proclaim their truths as self-evident ones. In all idealism, the petulance of '*Can't you see if only . . . !'* In all cynicism, the irritability of *'Stop fooling yourself . . . !'*

●

The *fact* of death is self-evident, but not its *content . . .* and even this *fact* of death relates primarily to *others.* Because death has been visited on all without exception it is still not absolute evidence it will be visited upon us – the source of medical imbecility and classical metaphor alike . . . (cults of immortality both . . .)

●

Death is the secret of secrets, the origin of the idea of the secret, of which desire is the highest manifestation *in life . . .*

●

The art of theatre, which recognizes in tragedy the greatest gift of the thinkers-of-death to the yet-to-be-dead, disposes of the self-evident with every gesture. In other words, it deems all acts both *possible* and *justified*, thereby countering the humanist slogan *'we are all human'* with the terrible riposte *'this is human also . . .'*

●

The art of theatre is a theatre *without limits*. It recoils from conscience as from any other constraint. It declines to apologize for the injuries inflicted by the *depravity* of its speculations. Who can witness such things without anxiety? But anxiety is its *privilege*.

❀

The adorable becomes the contemptible. What seduced repels. *The one's* diminishing stock of charms. But does love not understand the poverty of charm and consign it to the repertoire of beginnings? Or did he expect it to *cease at the beginning*?

❀

Is it possible that the dying, in their haste to become the dead, experience no benefit at all from the kindness of the still-living? That kindness dispensed by the still-living is experienced by them as *imbecility*?

❀

Is it not also possible that the distinction made between the ugly and the beautiful death might be a peculiarly vapid one from the point of view of the *dying*?

❀

Death renders irrelevant all that was relevant. Whilst this injures the still-living (the still-loving) might this not be one of death's *generosities*?

＊

So much left on the shore of death . . . how near does tragedy come to this *annihilation of values*?

＊

If death has a language it will not be our language. Tragedy anticipates the language of death, both in the speech and the *shock* of the speech. How could it fail to shock? It utters what has not been uttered. It *steals utterance from death* . . .

＊

Are the tragedians brave enough for the tragedy? Even in *the art of theatre*, the longing to recuperate value from the dying of values . . .

＊

Dracula – the fear of the *known*. He must come in the night, to the sleeping (unspeaking) one, when she can be imagined, when she cannot reveal her *appalling familiarity* by utterance. Is Dracula not characterized by fatigue?

Is he not the epitome of the lover who has heard it all, and for whom *the one* can be contemplated only as mute? Dracula – the exhaustion of the erotic repertoire.

*

The art of theatre exists for itself. How hard this is to say, to *mean*, hard because the prejudices of contemporary morality abhor 'things for themselves', demanding 'meaning' and 'use' in every *man* and every *thing*.

*

We speak too much of our *illegality*, as if we thought crime a distinction, when it is a poverty, a gesture of impotence. Rather, in *the art of theatre* we come to the audience not as criminals but as priests in a sacred art. But it is complicated. In its decay democracy charges the sacred with criminality.

*

He fell. He knew he was dying. She knew he was dying. In the instant of this knowledge everything that existed between them of love, history and intimacy was extinguished. In this fraction of time, the whole consciousness of the dying man reverted to himself, and if she were to recur, it could only be in the *retrospect* of death. Now, glimpsed through the veil of shock at his ending, she was alien to him as every other aspect of a world with which *he had no more to do*. The fragility of this bond, of *all bonds*, the essential disloyalty of things, struck him simultaneously with the profound physical damage that he knew at once was too strange, too profound to be mere *sickness* . . .

●

The horribly wounded soldier pleaded to be shot. He pleaded with the unwounded soldier to grant him the death that would end both his pain and his self-disgust. In the first look that passed between them, everything was communicated, not only the pity of the one for the shame of the other, but the ecstasy of the one *not to be* the other, even his *implication* in the ordeal of the other, an ordeal which alone made possible an exquisite sense of his own *health* (soon to be similarly shattered?) and therefore confirmed his malevolent participation in the random nature of death . . .

●

The theatre thus: '*let us describe what the audience feels. It will thank us for it*'. *The art of theatre* thus: '*let us describe what the audience does not know it feels. So what if it reviles us for it?*'

●

Lying and death. If death is in all things, is it not also in lying, which is the gesture par excellence of the *life-lover*, with his passion to master the world of facts, to re-arrange it, to be the supreme conjuror of things? In his impatience to evade the actual, the liar resembles a dancer and like a dancer he is susceptible to mortal exhaustion, for the *actual* will insist upon itself, leaning hard on his shoulders. But at the very moment the *fact of mortality* imposes itself upon this *denier of gravities*, is not *all* revealed as a lie, even the very facts he disputed? A sense of profound insignificance overwhelms the consciousness, since for the dying nothing possesses value. And now the liar might be regarded as a pitiful hero, one who found the world wanting long before death showed in truth *how wanting it was . . .*

❋

All I describe is theatre even where theatre is not the subject.

❋

The theatre resents *the art of theatre*, sensing its deeper intimacy with its public. All the lavish endowment of superficial skills and décor, the critical allegiance, the celebrity actors, the vulgar imprimatur of the patronage of the state with its palaces of art and its marketing bureaucracy (would you require to market a *need*?) cannot conceal the *unhealthiness* of the transaction. The intimacy that characterizes *the art of theatre* derives from the very condition *the theatre* is at such pains to eliminate – *anxiety*. In *the theatre* they talk of 'the show'. Does this not tell us everything about their condescension? But even they still possess sufficient modesty not to describe their efforts as *revelations* . . .

❋

Leave if you wish. Leave without barbarity, however. The fact of your leaving is of no interest to others. Above all, in leaving do not demonstrate you have *escaped*. If *the art of theatre* is a prison, it is one where the incarcerated *willed their ordeal* . . .

❋

In *the art of theatre* something is always *lost*. In a world of relentless aggregation, to lose might be a lightness, an intoxication. What is it that is lost? The burden of your moral convictions. This is a loss that might be experienced as a *privilege* . . .

❋

Ourselves and the deaths of others. How much can we say? That no amount of witnessing the *dying* of others prepares us for the experience of *death* in ourselves. Do these others – whilst *dying* – share a *death*, or do they experience *deaths* as variously as they experienced their lives? Conventional wisdom insists we are all equal at the grave, but is this not to *patronize* death from a perspective of unredeemed ignorance, since all that is reported is reported of *dying* and never of *death* . . . ?

●

What if there were a hierarchy of the dead? We know nothing . . .

●

The peace of the grave. So it seems from *outside* the grave. What if death were cacophony? We know nothing . . .

●

On *envying the dead*. Conventionally, misery causes me to envy the dead. We aspire to cease existing in *this place* – a paradox, since to lose consciousness of *this place* might only result in the transposition of our consciousness to another, *worse place*. We know nothing. Our misapprehension of death is derived from the silence of the cadaver, but *the cadaver is not death* . . .

●

Moments of profound sexual passion cause us – the couple who love – to implore a death, if only from the anxiety that nothing will ever again surpass the *unearthly* quality of this ecstasy. Is it not too perfect to be followed, except by its repetition? The dread of its failing to reappear . . . the yearning for its reappearance . . . perhaps the solitary reason for perpetuating ourselves?

●

Every day he woke he thanked God he was still alive, whilst knowing this relief was not itself proof of his enjoyment of life. Like most who possess a thing, he could not abandon even what he did not value. On the other hand, he was not sure that he had not deceived himself into thinking he did not value it only to safeguard himself against the pain of its loss . . .

●

How death makes idiots of us . . . in this it is the supreme *discipline* . . .

●

How tragedy restores an equilibrium – not by making an idiot of death, not by *turning the tables* (no amount of artistic investment can make the contest an equal one, even if death were, on close examination, *idiotic*) but by discovering *the means to enter it*. Let us not flatter ourselves that this is *dignity*. It has more of *fascination* than dignity can ever have . . .

●

Tragedy assures us that if Man cannot overcome the fatuous terms of his own existence he might overcome the fatuous apprehensiveness of its demise . . .

●

All tragedy entices death into showing itself. It tempts it into *doing its worst*. In doing so this worst is discovered to be less bad than we imagined. The greatest tragedy goes further. It makes of death a necessity, even a perfection, and not only for the old, the sick or the fatigued, but for the agile, the vigorous and the healthy. Is it possible to go further? To ask if death does not belong prima facie to the strongest?

●

Tragedy does not admonish, it seduces . . .

●

Tragedy is not a demonstration, it is a terrible ignorance that admits itself . . . a disarming naïveté clings to all its protagonists . . .

❧

If death were simply nothing we would fear it less and contemplate it less. The anxiety surrounding death arises from the possibility it is *not nothing*. This anxiety is fuelled by the rumour of its being *something*.

❧

The bereaved in their torment cling to preposterous delusions, finding comfort in such implausibilities as '*he knew nothing*' or '*she died instantly*'. The briefest examination of such platitudes reveals them to be meaningless. Whilst it is manifestly true that it takes a fraction of a second for a body to be disintegrated by a bomb, why do we insist on identifying the fragmentation of the flesh with the experience of dying, let alone the experience of *death*? The moment life ceases in the body may be a medical conundrum, and as such is best left to the banalities of the specialists. The question that concerns us in the sphere of spirituality is how death entered the consciousness of the disintegrated individual. To declare that '*he knew nothing*' is a worthless palliative. He *knew* everything. We must reiterate the appalling truth that only the dead can know the form of their dying . . .

Rest in Peace . . . why do we wish to bestow on the dead a condition of placidity we eschew in the world of the living? Should we not rather say *Rest in Knowledge*? But then we would envy them. There would be a rash of suicides . . . !

The art of the theatre knows nothing. It relegates knowing to *the theatre*, the place of commodities. In place of this knowing, it affirms the *integrity of fictions* . . .

The art of theatre holds evidence in contempt. Its propositions require no proof, nor are they susceptible to the trivializing objections of empiricism. It consigns all questions of proof to the realm of *prejudice*.

Life is experienced as a number of things, many contradictory. We do not know if death is not similarly complex. But, it will be objected, life and death are not simple antitheses (movement/stillness, noise/silence . . .). How loud is the silence of the grave? If death utters, it does so in a language learned only by the dying.

Dying – an education?

The one hated him. The discovery she hated him might under ordinary circumstances have convinced him she was not *the one*, but he was not a man to leap to conclusions. He slowly understood he hated her also, but that this hatred, far from being a reason for ceasing to love, was an aspect of its authenticity, even evidence of its *profundity.* That all men hated all women, and all women hated all men, seemed on reflection to be self-evident, and the ecstasies that distinguish great passion seemed to him to resemble those precious stones which, found only at great depth in the earth's crust, are formed of, encased in, and created by, the base material which surrounds them. He refined the notion – essential if he were to continue to believe she was indeed *the one* – that the rage and resentment she now openly showed him were futile acts of mutiny against an engulfing desire that overwhelmed her. The evidence of *one-ness* lay precisely in the vehemence with which she tried to demonstrate she was not *the one* at all . . .

We envy the dead nothing but their knowledge of what death is.

*

The art of theatre does not occupy itself with the amelioration of human existence. This alone distinguishes it from all other theatre practice, whose goodwill is a vulgarity. All that may come to be described as the *satisfactions of the art of theatre* are accidental, by-products of an ordeal . . .

*

The greatest mystery of the universe is death. Unlike other mysteries, the mystery of death is characterized by terror. Only tragedy makes death its exclusive concern. It therefore enters willingly into terror, without presuming to disarm it. More than ever tragedy is *necessity*, for we have passed through the extinction of religion only to encounter the extinction of science. Admire death for its disdain of these tranquillizing mythologies. Its obscurity is *impenetrable* . . .

*

To state it again. We are not speaking of *dying*. Even science has much to say about dying, the civilizing of dying . . . it is possible the doctors have seized *dying* from *death* . . .

●

We cannot be enlightened about death. Is it not a profound satisfaction to know there is one place at least immune from the *civilizers*? I called death a *place*. Even *I* wish to enlighten *myself* . . .

●

The art of theatre is a darkness, because it speaks to a darkness. How does it protect the wealth of its darkness from the enlighteners? How does it protect its darkness from its own will to abolish this darkness – for, let us confess it – there is no man alive who lacks the *compulsion to teach*? In the first instance we scrupulously cleanse ourselves of all those moral, medical and political neuroses pertaining to the *improvement of mankind*. We deny ourselves the coercive pleasure of *instructing the public*. The annexation of theatre as a platform for the conscience of the author we deem *barbaric*. Second, we discard all obligation except the supreme obligation to intensify the hazard of the performance, to the public and to ourselves alike. In this determination to imagine beyond the perimeters of experience *the art of theatre* reveals its absolute identity with the tragic form.

I think I do not wish to be dead. Even when I utter the phrase which most characterizes all the cultures and periods of human history – '*I wish I were dead*' – I cannot be certain I mean it, for what I mean by it is the desire to be *not here*, *not now*, and *nothing*, which may not be the condition of death, after all, we cannot know. A similar misapprehension attaches to heroic phrases such as '*I do not fear death*'. How can you have no fear of a thing you know nothing of? We patronize death. If death is monstrous, our bravado is pitiful. If it is innocuous, our dread is infantile.

•

If we were permitted to know death, which is perhaps not one thing, i.e. a thing common to all individuals who experience it, but is, like life, experienced differently by different individuals and *not a universal at all*, we might say '*I wish I were dead*' for the wish to have meaning. It remains, however, an exasperation with the *known*, and not an authentic desire for the *unknown*. Is this mortal exasperation not a condition for entering the tragic stage?

•

Only '*I love you*' surpasses '*I wish I were dead*' in the extent of its universality, even if it partakes of its ambiguity. With *the one* it was impossible to resist uttering the words even if – for reasons of the politics of love – he deemed it better to resist uttering them, precisely to provoke the demand that the words be said ('*Don't you love me any more?*'). He longed to hear the one plead for his affirmation. He withheld only to restore . . .

●

I have to be dead. Whatever death is, I must know it (whatever dead is, I must be it). I am therefore impatient, because the inevitable provokes impatience, as if a game of withholding were played with me, and my pride resented it.

●

He held between his fingers a photograph of *the one*. Not as she was. As she had been. Her childish hairstyle, simply drawn back and fixed in a grip, childish and yet as with so much that is childish, so swift and plain as to make dubious any subsequent hairstyle had improved on it, and her eyes, wide with some emotion that had also caused her jaw to fractionally drop, all pleasure and misapprehension . . . an image of the most intense life but also of death, as if it were published in a newspaper and she were a long-forgotten murder victim . . . but *the one* is not dead, she exists only in that miasma of *dreaded death* which causes the lover of the loved one to cry out with such heartfelt anxiety, '*Don't die . . . promise me . . . !*' And yet is this child – *the origin* of *the one* – not dead in fact, for nothing of her remains that can be seen here but a way of looking, *a soul* perhaps? Every material factor that contributed to the *one-as-a-child* has – by the law of cellular reproduction – been replaced many times and only the photograph remains, albeit decayed. He examined an image of one who existed once and existed no longer whilst certainly *continuing to exist . . .*

●

My darling . . . how distinct from the vacuous *darling* of even the most felicitous marriages . . .

My darling . . . how its utterance evokes the proximity of death, whilst being a forestalling of death, an appeal to death to stay its hand, as if so much love deserved *time . . .* the words cast a net over *the one . . .* yet was *the one* ever more frail than at the moment she was dedicated with these two words? Instantly she became unsafe (only his love could preserve her . . .).

My darling . . . the mother who seized her child from the jaws of an accident, smothering him in tears and kisses ('*how near to death you were . . .*').

●

My darling
Get out of my sight
My darling
GET OUT OF MY SIGHT

'Gertrude – The Cry'

The passionate possessive prefix which strips the word of its domestic aridity . . . a cultural password to *the art of theatre*, which takes all desire to the point of death . . .

*

By making death the sacred object of our meditations *the art of theatre* at once dispenses with the pitiful paraphernalia of *representation* that so disfigures the stage of *the theatre*, with its shrill and infantile assurances we are in a real place . . .

*

To *say all* – which is the manner of *the art of theatre*, just as it is unthinkable both in life and in the imitation of life that is *the theatre* – to vacate the unsaid by uttering it – is to liberate death onto the stage, for what is the unsaid if it is not death? The art of theatre is all-saying, therefore it is *death-saying* . . .

*

We who are not yet dead, but who must become dead, enter the room of the performance asking nothing of the actors but their *faith* (certainly not their *celebrity*, which is the sanitization of the imagination, and therefore demanded by *the theatre* . . .). But faith in what? To ask an actor for *faith*? But are these not the least faithful of all individuals, liars and outcasts since the beginning of time? Might it not be cruelly said of the actor that his soul is for sale? But *not* to demand it of him? We say *tragedy* cleanses the actor . . .

❦

To *stage death* we must — let us admit it, and affirm it — abolish the *critical regard* — a regard so fissured and cataracted as to have become in any case a *condition of the blind* . . .

❦

Should we not speak a simple truth? *Death is health to society.* And having spoken it, affirm that anxiety is an inextinguishable feature of existence. In its obsession with the elimination of pain, society *sickens* itself . . .

❦

The dead body is an object of fascination both in life and in art. What is more, its *decay* is mesmerizing. In theatre the living body must *represent* the cadaver, it cannot *imitate* it. To do this, it lies still. This little we know of death, and perhaps only this, that the dead *lie still* . . .

●

Because children play violent games, they also play at death. If they were forbidden to act violence, still they would play at death. In the child's game, to die is to become still (*'I shot you, lie down'*) and the playmate who mutinies against death is always reprimanded (*'But I killed you . . . !'*). Some of 'the dead' lie still a very short time before resuming the game (in another persona), an acceptable convention. Sometimes a single child lies still too long (*'Come back into the game . . . !'*) straining to imagine death (*'But I am dead . . .'*). This child is conventionally regarded as 'strange'. But it is his ecstasy . . .

●

Tragedy is never about *waste*, the source of the pain that surrounds the *accident* . . .

●

A sequence of horrors may be enacted on the stage without the least approximation to a tragedy. We have seen this, the excess of depravity that, taken as a residue, means nothing more than '*I hate my life . . .*'. Tragedy's engagement is with death, but from the deepest encounter with life . . .

❋

'*I am not yet dead.*' Of all the statements that could be made about existence, this is attended by the deepest apprehension . . .

❋

The significant question of the tragic narrative is this – how is death attained by the protagonist? Viewed from this perspective, all the tortuous manoeuvring of the plot is simply *prevarication* . . .

❋

The actor – who knows nothing of the facts of death (if death even belongs to the realm of facts) pretends to be dead (according to our infantile conception of the state of death), while we, equally ignorant, agree to admit this as at least symbolically valid ('*Good enough to be getting on with*', so to speak . . .).

❋

The profoundly revelatory aspect of tragedy is its recognition that *death argues* . . . the duration of this argument in the case of the tragic protagonist is his luxury and our privilege. But all death argues, even in the accident, even under the lorry wheels.

❊

'*We are telling you something . . . !*' the pathetic justification of second-order dramatists for staging their work. '*We are telling you nothing . . . !*' the discreet gesture of first-order dramatists unwilling to be *contaminated* by the function of the *educator* . . .

❊

'*We are telling you nothing . . .*', more precisely, '*we are telling you nothing you do not already know . . .*'. But *where* is it known?

❊

Whereas one knows death will occur (even if one hardly *believes* it will occur) one lacks the strength for its occurrence. So it is with the *representation* of death in the tragedy. We bring our anxiety with the inevitable encounter into the room. The success of the performance lies in making tolerable what we find intolerable, in making desirable what we only dimly sense *might be* desirable . . . we emphatically repudiate all notions of therapy or the moral categories in which the therapeutic drapes itself – despair, pessimism, celebration, for just as *the art of theatre* abolishes the utilitarian, it abolishes also the ethical. *The art of theatre* shrinks from the smothering embrace of the useful and the responsible as a sensitive child avoids the kiss of a noxious relative. It situates itself *beyond the question* . . .

●

The art of theatre replaces the question by the *vortex of desire*. We do not ask of a character *'should he have done that?'* He does what he does. We do not state *'she is unforgivable'*. She acts as she wills. To bring the habits of questioning to *the art of theatre* is to be lost at the out-set, rather as a stranger to a locality, unable to speak the language, substitutes for his ignorance by shouting . . .

●

We do not question death. Only a decayed humanism can question death (*'Should we die at all?'* or more fatuously but now commonplace, *'we should not die unnecessarily* . . .'). In tragedy we argue for *better terms* . . .

●

Our abhorrence of *the killing*, as if it were not a *natural cause*. The killing is the worst aspect of death to the living, an offence to culture. Yet it remains, *ab initio*, only a means of arriving at death. In life, as in tragedy, we suffer to hear how the individual came by his death. Always in theatre the speech reporting the killing commands a terrible silence, born of curiosity and dread ('*so that is how it happened . . .*') and the more outlandish the mode of the killing, the more rapt is the attention, but whereas in life we plead for consolation ('*she knew nothing*', '*it was all over in a minute*' and such fantasies) in tragedy we do not demand it, it would seem *demeaning*. In this fact alone we see the supreme gesture of tragedy, its *superiority* to the trivial compensations of the here and now, its proximity to the greatness of death as our final expression of anguish, and how this anguish – much to our astonishment – is superior to our pitiful longing for *peace*. How else do we explain the ecstasy of the martyrs?

*

'*Forgive my dying . . .*'. Could anything be more pitiful than this adieu of the loved to the stricken-with-grief? '*Forgive my dying*' not because you love me only, but because I am/have been the world as you knew it, and my absence (the first and last appreciable fact of death) alters your world, it is an injury done to your world, whatever your judgement of *me . . .*

Bereavement is an agony no amount of goodwill can alleviate. Tragedy understands this loss as absolute, a silence that must not be filled, but *visited*, as Aeneas visited Hell in order to suffer irredeemable loss . . .

●

Tragedy provides no healing for the silence of death – even the poetry of loss utters in a narrow register – its emotional resources have been exhausted in the coming-into-death of the dead one. Nothing remains for the survivors, who in any case are consigned to the chorus by the poverty of their continued existence . . . is there not a sense in which they are excluded from something (death . . .) and even diminished by their exclusion?

●

The melancholy of the tragic protagonist is the consequence of too-much knowledge. He already knows the world in its entirety, and nothing arrives in the form of a surprise, however much is *discovered* . . .

●

Whereas the tragic protagonist has abolished hope in himself, he is not without *inspiration*. This inspiration is born out of the last remnant of his naïveté – the conviction that at least death cannot be *the world repeated* . . .

●

Murder is the first door of tragedy, as suicide is the last (all the deaths of tragic protagonists are effectively, suicides . . .).

●

Murder is eternal, such an essence of human relations that it must be regarded as an expression of *life*, so proximate in our civil existence that it stands as an admonition against exaggerating the amiability of man . . .

●

Tragedy makes of murder its most creative instrument, the first gesture of re-ordering that dominates the spiritual revolution of the protagonists. In this sense it is a *grace* . . .

●

In desire the death-wish is momentarily suspended by the illusion that love might be more-than-the-world . . .

Behind every door – even the door of desire – the world is reproduced. Behind the door of death there is the possibility that this nauseating reproduction ceases. We cannot know.

●

If tragedy confronts that poverty of existence, it also challenges death to justify its significance, its scale of dread . . .

●

The estimate of the *value* of death rises with the intensification of the frustration of life. It has no stable value. On the other hand, death might possess *surplus* value – it might be *more* than silence, *more* than nothing . . . it might be a form of *something* (not being merely nothing . . .).

●

One need not share the tragic state (the state of too-much knowing) to receive tragedy. It is not so enclosed. One needs only the instinct that there *might be* too much knowing. Instinct lies at the heart of the tragic experience.

*

There is no innocent tragedy, only innocent accident. Yet is it not innocent to rage at the world for its inadequacy? Perhaps, but between the complacency of the stoic and the complacency of the social reformer, such an innocence acquires the status of the *perfectly human* . . .

*

In the world of *the theatre* life cannot be discerned to be either meaningless or inadequate. This very perception would disable its functions (for *the theatre* is pre-eminently functional). Characters possessed of such intuitions are consigned to the madhouse (the therapist . . .). In this alone we discern how close bourgeois theatre is to *the Soviets* . . .

*

No one in tragedy is a *case*. Tragic characters are *propositions*, not *conditions* . . .

*

We do not regret the death of the tragic protagonist. How can one regret what another requires? That this *is* a requirement is demonstrated by the play.

The utilitarian mind is enraged by this proof, for it cannot admit the necessity for death, even in its bitterest opponents. Why? Because all lives are equally *useful* in its eyes, as all lives were once equally *valuable* in the eye of God. What is more, to admit death willingly is a rebuke to *health*, and the utilitarian mind pursues health with a determination that alone demonstrates its profound *unhealthiness*.

●

The sordidity of *influence* . . .

●

The art of theatre repudiates the *will to influence* as a perversion shared by elements of *the theatre* as diverse as socialist realism and the Broadway musical (how diverse *are* these on close inspection?). Only in the abolition of *the will to influence* does *the art of theatre* begin to recognize itself . . .

●

The abolition of *function* and *influence* determines the *moral condition* of the production. In discarding the baggage of sordid ambitions that identifies *the theatre*

– the dispensing of 'truth', the 'correction of attitudes', the 'giving' of pleasure – *the art of theatre* creates an immunity for itself. An immunity from what? All *transactions* . . .

❋

In place of these transactions it elevates the *feeling for death*. . . . Is this to say it is a theatre that concerns itself only with death? Not at all. We say only that in the absence of a *feeling for death* nothing can be understood. Must all things be understood? Very well, let us express it precisely. In the absence of a *feeling for death* things can be neither *understood* nor *felt* . . .

❋

We cannot repeat it too often – *the art of theatre* does not seek an audience, it acquires one . . .

❋

The perversity of the social realists – as if seeing were believing . . . !

❋

My fear of death is the same as everybody's fear of death. But I make it a significant fear, a *valuable* fear, by admitting it even into pleasure. I welcome its contribution to ecstasy . . .

*

Does one elect to be a writer of tragedies? It is a seduction.

*

The one came to exemplify all that could no longer be evaded, she was therefore a *recognition* that what had seemed escapable was not, and as such, was relief from an enervating and pointless struggle. *The one* was a joyous yielding to the determinant facts, in other words, *the end of the world.* In this she possessed an awesome familiarity . . .

*

The one's uncanny ability to look/sound like the history of his race . . .

*

The one – the yielding of all claims . . .

*

Its disconcerting *closeness* despite the unfamiliarity of its themes . . .

Its knowing that our unknowing is a collective amnesis . . .

Its supreme naturalness in spite of its shocks, as if a light were suddenly thrown into a dark mirror and we saw in our terror a reflection, but the reflection was *us* (we had always been there . . .).

In talking of the already-there we can say *the art of theatre* has immanence . . .

Can one say '*this only seemed to be what I did not already know?*' (It came *disguised* as the unknown . . .).

Can we say further that in this coming to the already-known we must pass through a state of anxiety?

Can this be said to be the experience of death?

A proposition – nothing in death is not already known.

●

A further proposition – in *the art of theatre* the more we exert ourselves to abolish the real (the damage done to us by the *recognizable*) the nearer we approach the *known*.

●

Aristotle – the critical policeman confronted with death attempts to *arrest* it . . .

●

Aristotle's catharsis – death must be made *useful* . . .

●

Aristotle and tragedy – nothing too great that it cannot be annexed in the interests of social order . . .

●

Aristotle – forcing politics onto the supremely apolitical . . .

●

The profound *dread* in Aristotle . . . that the example of the tragic protagonist may be *infectious* . . . what if we also jumped over our lives?

*

Tragedy humiliates our innocence, a thing so contrived as to deserve its humiliation. In place of this false innocence, it introduces the authentic innocence of the suicide, an innocence preserved by death's *contempt for the collective*. Only the most febrile sexual encounters imitate such a depth of indifference . . .

*

Now the actress is dead let us examine the few remaining images of her, her films, her classic gestures. Already we discern the distorting effects of her disappearance on what seemed to be the eternal stability of photography. Was her every glance not filled with disappointment? And we described her as supremely *sexual* . . .

*

'*Kill for me* . . .' (Salome, Gertrude . . .). Love's infinite requirement for proofs . . . *killing* the supreme erotic gift . . . in passion, the insatiable appetite for sacrifice . . .

*

The impatience felt by the living for the slow-dying ... is this a cruelty, or has tragedy's way with dying – its gesture – made all reluctance an *artistic embarrassment*?

※

The humanist hyper-valuation of *all life* ('*we have achieved yet further longevity . . .*') reduces all cultural engagement with death to a spasm of *ingratitude . . .*

※

Death has no interest in how we die . . .

※

Dancing to the scaffold – spiritual poverty as bravado, the mortal equivalent of visiting a prostitute . . .

※

We who are not dead but who will be dead, inhabiting a world once filled with the now-dead, go to the place of death, which is not the mortuary or the graveyard (sites for the disposal of the *consequences of dying*) but the tragic theatre, which separates death from dying – an impossibility for those in the throes of death, who like those in the throes of birth, are consumed with *discovery . . .*

＊

In tragedy death can never be a *character* (was it not tragedy that abolished *Death* from the stage? Tragedy found it *beyond personification*, and revealed thereby its own essentially *irreligious* nature . . .).

＊

It is safe to say of the tragic character, he has a fascination with death. But let us go further and identify *death's fascination with him*. Is he not a death-seducer, and is death not flagrant with him?

＊

In removing the death penalty from its menu of punishments society announces that nothing in the sphere of mischief or criminality deserves death. In our instincts we nevertheless affirm there are many acts for which death alone can satisfy our offence, yet we forego this satisfaction. All the same, there is a nausea in this sacrifice. This nausea might be more sickening (socially, individually) than that which accompanies *the execution* . . .

＊

In the vortex of his crime the criminal experiences the ecstasy that accompanies all challenges to death. His act is an enticement to death, but it carries a moral power only where death is the penalty. The violation of women has from the darkest beginnings of human culture been a transgression in which death was a third party, not only for the victim – whose life is always at stake in sexual extremis – but for the perpetrator, whose act – dignified by the prospect of execution – invokes the *spirit of sacrifice* . . .

●

'*Two wrongs don't make a right.*' Ethical redundancy in tragedy.

●

The silence of death from the side of the still-living – we know nothing of the loudness of death from the side of the now-dead – is painful precisely because it is silent, it is the *end of the question* ('*I did not ask her . . . I will never know now . . . so much was unsaid . . .* ' etc.). Thus the dead pass into the realm of secrets. Is this not beautiful? Are we not maddened by the question, by the relentless *exchange*? The dead have ceased to *exchange* . . .

We must penetrate the secret. The secret craves penetration (*'Can you keep a secret?'*: a plea for its violation . . .). This restless activity of exposing the secret, and the bathos of the exposed secret, constitutes a secular religion . . .

'Let them die wondering . . .' (who I was . . .).

No metaphor for what is sublime in silence. If silence were a wall, one would seek a ladder for it. Rejoice in *one* absolute.

Smacking a dying man . . . *'he is escaping with his secret . . . !'*

The degeneration of the cadaver, its colours, its odours, its deliquescence . . . an admonition to desist from acts of life (*'I kissed her dead mouth, I held her dead fingers, I leapt into her grave . . .'*). The cadaver's insistence on the futility of the earthly gesture cannot be adduced as evidence that the dead have *moved* . . .

❋

Because the dead are beyond imagination, are they nowhere at all?

❋

'*I refuse to admit my incapacity to imagine it* . . .' But even your imagination is in *this* dimension . . .

❋

The tomb – simultaneously a hygiene and a statement of resistance by the still-living to the authority of death, a material gesture of the unconsoled, denial made concrete ('*Their names liveth for evermore*' – how we call up untruth in the rage of our resentment . . .).

❋

Tragic experience is never consolation, rather it compels an action from mourning itself . . . (to seduce the grieving widow . . .)

❋

In tragedy, death is not an opposite to beauty but a constituent of it — death's *pause* is beauty's *permission* . . .

❋

If all desire is for the unpossessed, the unfelt, the yet-to-be experienced, can we say of death that it is *desired*?

❋

Death as an object of desire (not death as an undesired consequence of a desire for another thing, e.g. power, another man's wife, a price reluctantly paid, but a mystery to be *violated* . . .).

❋

Death advertises the failure of all things, the decay of all projects, the corruption of all ideals. The tragic protagonist has allowed this to permeate his entire personality. His certainty that *nothing can last* produces in him a febrile, convulsive energy. It is true to say the same awareness in another might induce *lassitude* . . .

❋

The poet lay across the railway tracks. His life according to others (even poets . . .) was deemed *unsatisfactory* (he did not share their pleasures, he was not married, his poetry had no following . . .). All his life he had loved trains, but for their melancholy. It seemed certain he hated life but he might only have loved death *more* . . .

●

To love death . . . to love precisely what is *unknown*? Is it possible to speak to loving what is unknown (i.e. nothing? To love the *appearance* of nothing, for it cannot simply *be* nothing . . . ?). To love death must be to love the possibility of something which declines to reveal itself except upon an irreversible decision.

●

The boy of six sat beside *the one*, he wished to be alone with *the one*, not only now but forever, even at six he understood *forever* as intimately bound up with *the one* but they were not alone, they were surrounded by others, by idiots, by well-wishers, by the dutiful, and she, oh, how little she seemed to share his longing for their exclusivity, she talked freely, she laughed noisily, she swung her legs on her stool, *she wanted things to happen to her*, her long hair curled over her white collar, over her chequered dress, and she ate, she *ate* things from the table, cakes, jelly, sandwiches, whereas he ate nothing, he could not eat at all nor understand how she could if she were *the one*, a hatred filled his mouth instead, for her, for all of them, *the one* was no less an idiot than them, what could save her, nothing, he knew at six she never could be saved and yet she breathed her wholesome life, she exuded life and drew life to her whereas he shrank, he felt himself diminishing, was she not twice his height, it was preposterous, a mismatch, she was *the one* but still a *mismatch*, laughter burst around him, one of the idiots had told a joke, she laughed, *the one* laughed at the idiot's joke and yet her laugh was false, he saw in her strange eyes she laughed for no reason, and if she laughed for no reason she was perhaps afraid, afraid to show herself not laughing, and this fear made him certain that after all she was *the one*, and they possessed their fear in common . . .

•

Death – the end of certain conversations, but also *styles* of conversing, even *performances* of them . . .

•

The criminal

'*I am sorry for what I did, but only from this point of view, that had I known death was the consequence I should not have done it . . .*'

The heroic criminal

'*I am not sorry for what I did, I felt compelled to do it, and*

77

	if death is the consequence, I don't protest . . .'
The tragic protagonist	*'I am unforgivable, and if the consequence of my act had not been death I should never have undertaken it . . .'*
The criminal	*'I did it to impress others . . .'*
The heroic criminal	*'I could not deny myself the ecstasy of doing it . . .'*
The tragic protagonist	*'I did it to be revealed to myself . . .'*
The criminal	*'Give me another chance . . .'*
The heroic criminal	*'I am content to die . . .'*
The tragic protagonist	*'If you gave me more life I should throw it back in your face. Do you think I did this to be forgiven?'*

●

It is not impossible our mortal existence can be prolonged indefinitely, a body so repaired as to be without integrity, a *mobile cadaver*, an amalgam of derelict parts stolen from others, an apotheosis of the democratic dream of *absolute interchangeability*. What is the consequence of this *salvage* on the *tragic regard*? Is it not condemned to ever-deeper illegality?

●

'*I am exhausted with the relentless extension of my existence*' says the thousand-year-old man whose body is an altar of sacrifice (he gave his eyes, she gave her liver, they gave their limbs that he might endure until . . . until . . . *an explanation had been arrived at*?). To disdain our mutuality will become an offence only the tragic character will *rejoice in* . . .

●

Surgery versus tragedy . . .

●

The surgeon does not know pity any more than the lawyer knows truth – they are tradesmen distinguished by one thing – the *incapacity to imagine*. Is it not time to strip them of their pretensions to *philanthropy*?

Dying societies laugh . . .

It is healthy to laugh says the satirist — on the contrary, we are poisoned by it.

The mayor was knifed in his own carnival. Some said this was appropriate . . .

To repudiate laughter is not to become miserable. Tragedy is not *miserable*.

They dare to suggest — the laughter-makers — that without them we should become depressed. Tragedy is not *depressing*. Since tragedy is situated in the world of death we cannot avoid the conclusion therefore that *death is not depressing* . . .

Grief is terrible but not depressing. *'He leapt into her grave.'* Was this *depression*?

●

What was, and is, and forever must be, cannot be *depressing*. Depression is the failure of spirit. Who are the most depressed? The comedians. Fear is their territory. Tragedy fears nothing, it enters in, it must enter in, it senses this entering as an *ecstatic obligation* . . .

●

The art of theatre is characterized by impatience, as all that takes existence seriously recoils from trivia, lying and *consolation* (*'You take yourself too seriously'* – was there ever a more shameful rebuke, issuing as it does from a withering *modesty* . . . ?). This impatience ensures the highest values in the staging of the performance, since it is exasperated by imperfection . . .

●

No one pretends society does not need its ranks, its orders, its tablets of laws, its admonitions, its amnesias, its pathetic choruses, its preposterous teachers, its grinning governors, its unrevealing revelations, its fatuous debates; we state only that the tragic protagonist utters in his extremity the horror of the fact he is *condemned to society*, and that death alone is the exit. What he cannot know is whether death is a society also . . .

●

Do they *blame* tragedy? But it takes the blame . . . !

●

The one kills . . . how did he come to recognize this? At what point did the ecstasy of affirming *the one* was indeed *the one* resolve itself into a placid accommodation, an unresisting submission to the implacable nature of the fact *the one kills*? But it was obvious, and hardly had the idea lodged in him than it became unassailable, beyond the influence of will and the pitiful squirming of self-preservation. This gift of fatality in *the one* was simply a deeper stratum of desire, strangely silent but the silence born of *depth*, as if in a great castle, he had found floor under floor, crypt under crypt, and the sheer weight of the masonry stifled every instinct to escape. *The one kills* . . . could he tolerate death at the hands of anyone less?

●

A word to the necrophiliac – '*Because the cadaver is nothing, you have seduced <u>nothing</u>, nor violated <u>anything</u>.*' The necrophiliac – '*Someone must be there . . . !*'

Necrophilia – death as a cosmetic?

Necrophilia – a fine point in decay . . . a connoisseurship?

The necrophiliac – '*I do not ask for responses, but my act is informed by the memory of responses . . .*'

The suicide declines to exist under the conditions available to him; or, disdains to try to improve the conditions he finds intolerable. (We make no judgement of this disposition.)

By contrast, the will with which the tragic protagonist elects death is characterized by an overflowing impatience . . . he does not yield to death, as it were to a physician, he shakes death with what he *demands* of it . . . the possibility therefore of a *further tragedy* beyond his dying . . .

It is an illusion to think the tragic protagonist *makes mistakes* (pursuing 'wrong' ends, for example . . .) because his only end is death, his only dilemma, *how to arrive* at it. Only sociological criticism talks of 'tragic flaws' . . . a notion derived from the musty storehouse of the 'perfectability of man . . .'.

●

In tragedy, the redundancy of homely wisdoms . . . '*the wages of sin are death*' . . . '*we are born astride the grave*' . . . perhaps, but death and the grave are precisely where we *begin* . . .

●

The tragic protagonist is not tired of life, nor thwarted, both conditions which provide pretexts for *evasion* (and are the substance of the play of *the theatre* . . .). On the contrary, he has an *excess of existence* to his credit, both of a material and spiritual kind (authority, sexuality, imagination). It is true to say of the tragic character that he *lacks nothing* – unlike in the political play, lack is not the material of the drama, nor is it the source of his contempt. He might alter everything to his will (becoming a 'good' king) but such considerations are irrelevant to one who seeks, and is sought by, *death* . . .

●

Tragedy makes art from contradiction by substituting will and curiosity for dread and ignorance . . . in the field of *death* . . .

❋

If dying is an ordeal (it *appears* to be an ordeal . . .) is it possible to speak of a recovery? (Only the dead know . . .)

❋

Grief – how we recover from the dying of others. Grief as the expulsion of the dead from presence to memory (neither more authentic than the other . . .).

❋

The general condition of mankind – fear. In tragedy, the relegation of fear to the perimeters. Hence the origin of the resentment induced by tragic characters in the public, whose addiction to *the mirror* is itself a symptom of terror . . .

❋

Pity – a commodity in the demos ('*give us your money* . . .') but just as the body of the prostitute is never immune to love so pity might be discovered in an

uncorrupted form, thus in *the art of the theatre* we take
is as axiomatic that the public must declare '*I pitied where
I least expected to*'. Not in spoiled innocence, not in the
accumulation of misfortune but in an *obduracy* . . .

•

The abolition of values in *the art of theatre* allows a
mutiny of pity against the drill of the moral police . . .

•

Tragedy shrinks from empathy, disdains sympathy and
recoils from all the pseudo-emotions of realism in *the
theatre*, practices designed to generate the fatuous complacency of *identification* or *recognition*. To announce,
as the audience, '*I identified with him*' – a mark of
failure . . .

•

The tragic actress persuades you of her moral nakedness,
a nakedness which is paradoxically, an *obstacle to love*.
Never beyond the human, she describes the *possibility*
within the human, repudiating the sordid practices of
reproduction of the known, the familiar, the stereotypical.
In this she privileges herself as *desirable*, consequently a
challenge to the *likeable* . . .

From this moment on – *the remainder of my life* . . .

In the first focusing of the infant – *the remainder of his life* . . .

The man murdered in the doorway of his home, or exploded on the battlefield . . . swiftly, the redundancy of anger or ethics . . . he is already *somewhere else* . . .

Hamlet's father – a resentment ascribed to him by the *living* . . . his speech written in the language of the *yet-living* . . .

The presumption of the living in speaking of the dead ('*He would have liked* . . .'). Has death not altered him? Is not alteration the *hope of death*?

The tragic protagonist, were he dragged screaming to his execution, pouring out relentless accusation against others, or rebuking the cruelty of disease, would cease to be a hero of tragedy, for he cannot *dissent from his apotheosis* . . .

*

Let us repeat that this is not a madman's contempt for death, a futile effort of outbidding, for the tragic character feels the weight of death, he does not diminish it, least of all does he *ironize* it; he embraces death as the only way of relinquishing the unsatisfactory nature of existence (a measured rebuke to God, if there were God . . . ?).

*

Notwithstanding this, the possibility death is *unworthy of his gesture* . . .

*

He might enter death to find it as vulgar as a fairground, as banal as a holiday, *more life than life* . . .

*

What more stupefying bathos than for the tragic character to encounter in death the Christian God, let alone His son? Neither punishment (the father) nor forgiveness (the son) could diminish his contempt . . .

*

The gesture of tragedy is so sublime as to make the prospect of judgement unthinkable . . . (in this it is most distinct from history, where the will-to-judgement is inextinguishable . . .)

*

Life thinks only in terms of life, such that death can only be conceived as further life of a different order ('*He departed* <u>*this*</u> *life* . . .'). Might life be thought in terms of death?

*

The suicide who utters his longing '*to be out of it*' unwittingly poses the idea life has an 'outside', i.e. a place beyond life. Such habits of thought permeate even the most rigorous materialist consciousness.

*

'*I wish you dead*' . . . I might then state categorically no other can possess you, our love was eternal (it was not modified by any other), my solitude is endowed with a dignity it could never possess had I been *abandoned* . . .

⁕

'*This is so awful it is almost funny . . .*', an irony impossible in tragic art which knows nothing of *detachment . . .*

⁕

The appetite for identification, which characterizes *the theatre*, has no place in tragedy, where the death of the protagonist is *perfection*, i.e. never a cause for tears . . . debased democracies make tears the *lingua franca of collectivity* ('*See how human I am*' says the weeping politician, '*I'm just like you . . .*').

⁕

The peculiar impatience for death discernible in the very old is matched only by the peculiar impatience of the not-yet very old for them to *die* . . . the repulsion felt by the witnesses of this slow coming-to-death does not originate in physical decay but in the appalling know-ledge that '*none of it matters really . . .*': one of the few secrets in the world that no one wishes to be party to . . .

We sense the need to live *full lives*, to *fulfil ourselves*, even to experience *excess*, not in order to gratify ourselves but in order that during the ordeal of dying we shall not reproach ourselves with a haunting inventory of undone acts . . . but one who had not lived at all in the conventional sense, the possessor of powers he was indifferent to (he made love to no one, he owned nothing, he went nowhere . . .) might enter death without the least apprehension, since the spurious concept of fulfilment – like the acts of contrition so beloved of the religious – are only aspects of the *life-system*, irrelevant to and, dare one say – incomprehensible under – the altered conditions of *death* . . .

•

'*When I die I shall go somewhere* . . .' one of the foundations of Western culture . . .
'*When I die I shall go nowhere* . . .' one of the foundations of Western culture . . .
Neither of these statements is verifiable.

•

The art of theatre is both more ordered and more chaotic than its authors. Since it was liberated from the obligations of realism it finds meanings both in its form and in its content. *The theatre* by contrast can suggest no more than it is provided with, it is miserably *accident-proof* . . .

●

The theatre's dread of autonomy . . . *the art of theatre*'s evaluation of autonomy into a *principle* . . .

●

Autonomy's abhorrence of morality . . .

●

A vocabulary for *the art of theatre* . . .

> Infinite
> Functionless
> Intractable
> Nowhere
> Incalculable
> Illogical
> Arbitrary

Are these not the attributes of death?

●

Christ – whose reluctance to die disqualified him as a tragic hero were he even thought to be a candidate for such – at last finds life irksome, others irksome, himself irksome, but has committed his existence to a project of human reformation he now lacks the courage to repudiate . . . in this he is a perfect *son* but an uninteresting *man* (did he even wish to be a man . . . ?). By contrast to this *enervating loyalty* the tragic hero keeps faith in the air, a subject (one of many . . .) for speculation. He is the supreme conjuror of *concepts, values, prejudices* . . .

＊

In the fall of the tragic protagonist we witness therefore the *exhaustion of the conjuror* . . . in this spectacle we are privileged to know the supreme law of limitations but simultaneously to be *ecstatically uneducated by it* . . .

＊

The failure of even the tragic character to overcome the gravitational pull of all things, the impossibility of sustaining his conjuring of values, does not educate us against his arts. Let us repeat: *Tragedy is not a warning.*

＊

The seduction of the secret in *the foyer itself* – '*I did not like her immorality*' (spoken . . .). '*I would give anything to possess her will*' (unspoken . . .). The public game of the foyer is the coda to all dramatic art (the foyer being the rally of the party faithful . . .). Here opinion is official, but opinion is the enemy of tragedy . . . the *foyer after the tragedy* therefore . . . a casualty station for the moralists . . . ?

●

In relation to death we are all gamblers, for every exercise of will is subject to ridicule (the train crash, the haemorrhage . . .). It is tragedy's contempt for the accident that distinguishes it not only from the conventions of realism but from the chaos of existence itself. In its seduction of death, it *arranges* death as a lover might adjust the veil of his bride, so she might be *seen to advantage* . . .

●

The play of *the theatre* asks *how shall we live*? The tragedy asks *how should we die*? But where is the antithesis, for the tragedy answers the question *how shall we live* in the very act of exposing the way into death. It draws death back into life, and consequently *alters life* . . .

Is dying immune to the liar? Have we not known those who even dying *put on an act*?

●

It is absurd to convict tragedy of hyperbole ('how could such a speech be delivered by a dying man?') since it abolishes the real at the outset. It is equally absurd to think the dying lack their rhetoric, even where articulation is denied them. Is it not the privilege of *the art of theatre* to *give voice*?

●

The dead – consigned to insignificance. But for the dying, *the living consigned to insignificance* (he turned his face to the wall . . .).

●

Let us admit the poverty of all death-writing, as against love-writing, sex-writing, politics-writing. The only equivalence in poverty is *womb-writing* . . . (but this we *have* known . . .).

●

The source of the humanist's resentment of the tragic character – she is no one's *victim*. Humanist art thrives on the *victim*, for in the absence of victims there is no *shame* . . .

●

A *decent death* . . . in humanist society, the prerogative of anaesthetics . . .

●

Tragedy eliminates conscience from the stage, and for *no political purpose* . . .

●

The humanist's reluctant concession that conscience may be *suspended* for a *political* end . . .

●

Tragedy – to rejoice in being unforgivable even by those who long to be injured in *order to forgive* . . . (the peculiar moral dysentery of the humanist . . .).

Tragedy's a priori – that we live only to be destroyed by life – renders the notion of *wrong decisions* meaningless. *A right decision*, by extension, is equally untenable. It remains to be said that the decisions of the tragic character have value only in so far as they enable him to enter the unknown in a condition of *active acquiescence* . . . (neither '*I don't want to die*' nor '*so what if I die*' but '*nothing can keep me here . . .*').

●

The greatest challenge to the tragic actor is to *rid himself* . . . of what? *His desire to be loved*. So few are capable of this self-denial, which to be achieved must simultaneously deny *us* the satisfaction of recognizing his culture, his charm, his love of animals, his suitability for honours, etc. . . . .

●

To the actor – do you not understand we shall like your contempt for liking?

To the actor – do not try to be loved *despite* your character. Be envied *because* of your character (the inexplicable attraction of the *facts* . . .).

The tragic character is susceptible neither to *expediency* nor *tactics* (frailties which would identify him as *wistfully* human . . .). Where he remains *profoundly* human is in his instinct for domination – not of others, which would render him merely *political* – but of self. The enervation of this effort at absolute autonomy destroys him. But we yearn for his destruction. Can we tolerate the one who makes of solitude a superior place?

The tragic character – the despair of the psychoanalysts . . . nothing is *repressed* . . .

Of death we know nothing, of dying we know little except that which can be discerned in the dying, and this perhaps so far distorted by our perspective as to be evidence of nothing at all. All that can be said with certainty of dying is that the area of common consciousness shared with the yet-living diminishes and that these changes enhance some aspects of sensibility and diminish others. In this sense it might be said of the tragic character that he experiences the *moral condition of dying* at the apogee of his vitality (the disintegration of common consciousness, the decay of values, the collapse of hope . . . everything in him is a *taking-away* . . .).

●

The *need* for tragedy (we have established its *uselessness* . . .) consists in our witnessing the tragic character's rebuke to the nausea of existence. His supreme gesture is to repudiate the contract under which the fear of death governs the living of life. But what if – having found life insufficient – he discovers death insufficient also? (i.e. death fails to be *nothing* . . . ?)

●

No pagan or Christian character entering the after-life describes it in terms of disappointment. Only we dare contemplate the *inadequacy* of paradise . . .

●

Death enters, retreats and re-enters society as it enters and re-enters the individual life, sometimes marginal in its effects, sometimes a deluge. It can be denied for only so long, since in its long silences it becomes a subject of *longing* (the death-wish attaches to the condition of peace, do we recognize this now . . . ?).

❋

It must be admitted that the onset of plague, war and famine does not exalt the tragic experience, rather the opposite. Because the apocalypse renders routine all that is terrible, it extirpates the meditation that permeates all tragic action. In such conditions tragedy gives way with grace to antic comedy . . .

❋

All art shrinks from the competition of the real, and this is not to describe a shortcoming, but to admit a frailty. Tragedy exalts will as its ecstasy, desire as its principle, whereas the apocalypse renders will into memory, nostalgia, even *effeminacy* . . .

❋

The art of the apocalypse, the art of death unwilled, of death inflicted and not embraced, of coercion, of life robbed not yielded, of death as only one iota of universal slaughter, is a victim's art, one of pity therefore, or of indignation that this *need not have been*. In tragedy, there are no victims, only *sacrifices* . . . hence, the redundancy of indignation in *the art of theatre* . . .

❋

Only the most ruthless intellectual effort enables one to recognize

The dead are dead.
All that was said by the dead relates only to the life
lived by the dead.

❋

'*My death will haunt you* . . .' The threat of the ill-loved, a calculation whose succulence lies precisely in our ignorance of what death is, yet always susceptible to the riposte '*Who could resent the gratification death evidently holds out for you?*'

❋

The tragic character manipulates not only the private but also the public attributes of death – its *collective disciplines* – for death has not only been co-opted as a punitive instrument of the social order (the now defunct 'death-penalty' . . .) but we must now recognize that the *domestication of death* is the ideological foundation of the democratic system (the sickly obsession with health and consequently, *longevity* . . .). In abandoning his life, the tragic character shows his contempt for the collective neurosis. In this he has unwittingly acquired political significance . . .

●

To be killed by *the one* . . . or more likely, to suffer a death that could not have occurred without *the one*, and for *the one* to be universally held to be *unworthy* of the sacrifice . . .

●

He had to have her (he could not *not* have her . . .) but she was fatal to him. He concluded from this he had lost the will to live. But had he invited her as a consequence of losing the will to live? Had he mistaken her *one-ness*, at least to this extent, that lacking the will to live he might have bestowed the character of *the one* on anybody, that it was arbitrary which individual was called *the one*, since her only qualification for being *the one* was her suitability to be the agent of his extinction?

●

There must be a knife . . . if there is to be sacrifice, there must be a knife . . . the possibility however that only on glimpsing the knife does the sacrifice recognize his eligibility . . .

＊

'*I intend to kill you. I value neither my own life nor yours.*'

'*You ought not to kill me. I have hardly lived yet.*'

'*To whom does it matter that your estimation of the proper duration of your existence is about to be frustrated?*'

'*It matters to my parents, my lover and my friends. We live in the love of others as an embryo floats in the waters of the womb.*'

'*Exactly so. And in the same way your death will be suspended in the grief of others . . .*'

＊

The theatre gratifies when it gives no more than is expected of it . . . *the art of theatre* gratifies when it violates the tolerance of its public (is this not a contradiction? But the effects of the work of art are characterized by *delay* . . .).

＊

The problem is not to make the audience *critical* (the collective sigh of orchestrated dismay . . .) but *hazardous* . . .

●

Like the old woman who shortens her walk with every passing day *the theatre* is afraid to quit the moral perimeters of the domestic . . . but this house stinks . . . ! You must get fresh air . . . !

●

The theatre . . . its habit of masquerading as *the art of theatre* . . . and this is not always mischievous . . . let us say of *the theatre* – the cruellest verdict – *it does not know itself* . . .

●

A confession – even the tragedians have not yet adequately served their theme. In meditating on death they have been satisfied with metaphors of numbing poverty . . .

●

To die . . . to go into the darkness . . . if it *is* darkness . . . to go to the river . . . if it *is* a river . . . but alone and without the illusion of love . . . naked and *disastrously free* . . . this is the condition of the tragic character . . .

●

It is impossible – now, at this point in the long journey of human culture – to avoid the sense that pain is necessity, that it is neither accident, nor malformation, nor malice, nor misunderstanding, that it is integral to the human character both in its inflicting and its suffering. This terrible sense tragedy alone has articulated, and will continue to articulate, and in so doing, make *beautiful* . . .

●